One

MW01520042

Charles Robertson

Published by

Bottle Tree Productions

DEDICATION

Dedicated to Charlynne & Justin

One Act Plays for Kids were plays that were developed in our acting classes for kids at Bottle Tree Productions. Parts have been written for kids from six up to twelve years of age. There are four plays ranging from a brave Princess who must fight dragons to save her kingdom to an underwater adventure starring a lost school of Guppies to a Gnome uprising in Norway to a magical collection of Toys who come to life to save two little girls.

The plays all spring from the imagination of young children. The plays can be as simple in set design as a bare stage or as elaborate as imagination allows. Costumes, too, can be elaborate or simple. These plays provide good parts for all children involved. Many of the parts are gender neutral. Ranging from a play with parts for seven kids up to a play involving 20 kids, there are various options in this collection for different-sized casts.

These plays do not speak down to kids. These plays speak for kids.

Charles Robertson, April 2013

CONTENTS

ACKNOWLEDGMENTS

Special thanks to Anne Mariee for taking a leap of faith and pulling me kicking and screaming out of the stone age and a big Thank You to all the actors that have helped shape my work so positively.

One Act Plays for Kids

KING HECTOR THE HORIZONTAL

A story of a brave princess who climbs a mountain to slay a dragon and save the kingdom

GUPPY GETAWAY

An underwater fantasy about life under the sea for a school of guppies who get lost in the ocean

NIGHT OF THE GNOMES

Four garden gnomes rise up in rebellion against their human masters.

TOYS IN THE CLOSET

Toys in the Closet speaks to the imagination in all children-The idea that their toys are alive

One Act Plays for Kids

King Hector the Horizontal

by

Charles Robertson

Charles Robertson
KING HECTOR THE HORIZONTAL
A story of a brave princess who climbs a mountain to slay a dragon and save the kingdom

Characters

The Narrator

King Hector-A very lazy King

Queen Anika-His scheming wife

Daniella-The Queen's Lady-in-Waiting

The Grand Vizier-A wicked man

Princess Madelina

Colin-A baby dragon

KING HECTOR THE HORIZONTAL

(There are three thrones-This represents the palace. The first throne is large, the second is medium-sized and third is small. To one side of the stage is a large nest with a cardboard egg. This represents the mountain. The smaller thrones are empty. In the larger throne sits King Hector lying on his side)

The Narrator-*(Enters)* In a land far away in time and place there lay the tiny landlocked kingdom of Wobaggoneestoppeeland. You might not find the name of the kingdom in any history books or on any maps. But I assure you, it did exist. Today, it is better know as Switzerland. Much of this mountainous land had been infested with dragons, and much carrying off of villagers had ensued. The king of this little known kingdom was Hector the third, more commonly known as King Hector the Horizontal. Queen Anika was looking for a divorce.

Queen Anika-*(Enters-followed by her lady-in-waiting. Her lady-in-waiting is attempting to attach a crown to the Queen's head. The queen pulls out a sword and sneaks up behind King Hector with the intention of stabbing him)*

King Hector-*(Slowly gets up and surveys the kingdom)* Another Royal day *(He yawns and lies back down just as Queen Anika stabs at the empty space where the king's head had been)*

Queen Anika-Drat! I missed.

Lady-in-Waiting-*(Cheerfully)* But you tried your best your majesty. That's what counts! I hear poisoning works quite well. You could poison his strawberry muffins.

Queen Anika-*(Nods)* He does love his strawberry muffins.

King Hector-Oh wife. Where is our daughter?

Queen Anika-*(Looking around for somewhere to put the sword)*

King Hector-Oh wife!

Queen Anika-*(Suddenly puts the sword under the throne. She then gets up, fixes her hair and smiles)* Coming dear. What are you bellowing for?

King Hector-Come, come. Sit down beside me. *(The Queen sits in her medium-sized chair. Her lady-in-waiting fusses with her hair)* Where is our daughter; Princess Madelina?

Queen Anika-Doing her studies I expect. Deportment, table manners and curtsying. She will be queen some day and she has to learn how to be a queen. Being a queen is hard work. Do my nails. *(Lady in Waiting does so)* Its about keeping up appearances.

King Hector-Right you are. Take me for example. It's hard maintaining this image of a caring, hardworking king. *(King lies with his face hanging over the throne and his feet up over the back of the throne)*

Queen Anika-Yes of course.

King Hector-Where is my Grand Vizer?

Grand Vizier-*(Entering)* I am here! I am here! I am really here!

King Hector-Must you always be so irritatingly exuberant?

Grand Vizier-What can I say? I love my job. The palace intrigue, the plots to kill the king, the dragons in the mountains, the peasants are...

King Hector-Whoa there mister! Did you say something about plots to kill the king?

Grand Vizier-*(Looks at Queen Anika who glares at him)* Perhaps I spoke a little prematurely. After all, you're not dead yet.

King Hector-Right you are. I'm alive and... *(Kicks his feet)* kicking! What other news do you have for me Vizier?

Grand Vizier-Grand Vizier. Grand. I have a grand in front of my name and it makes me feel like a million bucks.

5

Charles Robertson

Queen Anika-Fool, do you have any other news?

Grand Vizier-Yes, ma'am, the peasants are revolting.

King Hector-You're absolutely right! They are disgusting! *(Yawns)* They are so lazy.

Grand Vizier-No sire. What I mean is something very different. They are preparing to march on the palace. They want to overthrow you. They have demands.

King Hector-But my people love me.

Queen Anika-They love you as I do.

King Hector-What are these demands?

Grand Vizier-They demand better housing conditions, better wages.

King Hector-We pay them?

Grand Vizier-And they want the dragons exterminated.

King Hector-Send out the army to crush the people!

Grand Vizier-The army has joined the people sire!

Queen Anika-And I want a bigger throne!

King Hector-Take this down.

(The Grand Vizier takes out a feather pen and begins writing on his scroll)

King Hector-We shall pay the people a stipend! A stipend I say! We shall put roofs over their heads and we shall send a party out to hunt the dragons.

Grand Vizier-As you wish sire.

King Hector-Where is my daughter?

Princess Madelina-*(Entering)* Here father.

King Hector-*(Whispers to The Grand Vizier)*

Grand Vizier-Your highness, your father wishes you to go and slay the dragons that live in the mountains.

Princess Madelina-But what about the army?

King Hector-*(Again whispers to The Grand Vizier)*

The Grand Vizier-His majesty's armies have mutinied. They have joined with the people and wish to overthrow the government. Someone needs to slay the mountain dragons. That someone is you.

Princess Madelina-But isn't that dangerous?

King Hector-*(pauses for a moment and then speaks again to the Grand Vizier)*

Charles Robertson

The Grand Vizier-His majesty insists it is no more dangerous than jumping off a cliff.

Princess Madelina-But I can't fight a whole dragon by myself.

Queen Anika-Yes, you're quite right my dear. You may take Daniela, my lady-in-waiting. I'm sure she'll be very useful. She can do your hair for you and advise you on what accessories to take with you. And don't worry about your father, we will take good care of him won't we Mister Vizier?

(The two of them laugh evilly and King Hector looks around nervously. They stop laughing and then laugh again.)

Princess Madelina-Don't I need some sort of weapon?

Queen Anika-*(Reaches under the throne and pulls out the sword she had hidden there)* Here, and don't come back, til the dragon's are dead, all of them. Bring us their wings! Have fun. Ta ta!

Princess Madelina-*(Looking at the sword and holding it awkwardly)* I have never used a sword before. Come on Daniela. *(She waves forlornly and leaves)*

Queen Anika-But wait! I need to have a word with my lady-in-waiting.

Daniela-*(Leaves the princess waiting for her at the exit as she returns to talk to the Queen)* Yes my queen?

Queen Anika- *(Draws her lady-in-waiting away from the others)* If a freakishly tragic accident were to befall the princess, I would be much in your debt. The mountains are high and steep. A sudden fall would be unfortunate but accidents do happen. Dragons are vicious fire-breathing creatures. If she were to accidentally burn up, it would be unfortunate, but accidents do happen. If you were to accidentally stab her in the heart, that would be unfortunate but accidents do happen. When you get back, *(Points at King Hector who laughs nervously)* this bumbling fool of a king shall be no more.

Queen Anika/Daniela-*(laugh evilly followed by The Grand Vizier-Finally, King Hector joins in)*

Daniela-Your wish is my command. *(Exits)*

Queen Anika-Such a nice young woman. I think I like her. Always eager to please. *(King Hector, Queen Anika and the Grand Vizier freeze or move in slow motion. They must act in a non-distracting manner and make no noise so that the audience will not become distracted when action focuses on the mountain scene)*

The Narrator-Meanwhile, up in the mountains, a young dragon was hatching.

9

Charles Robertson

(In the nest, the cardboard egg cracks as Colin comes out making baby dragon sounds-He tries to flap his wings and falls over)

The Narrator-His name was Colin. How do does your humble storyteller know this? Because all dragons of Wobaggoneestoppeeland were called Colin. Adult dragons did not care for their young. They simply laid their eggs and vanished. Because of this, young dragons rarely had to go to school, or babysit their little brothers. Baby dragons could not fly. At least not for up to two years of their young lives.

Colin-*(flaps his arms and looks pathetic)* Mama? Papa? *(He then looks very sad before looking up at the sky)* Bird...Bird...Bird...*(Jumps up and down futilely. Colin looks momentarily depressed)* Bird gone. *(Obviously watches something hop)* Bunny....Bunny...Bunny. *(Tries to slowly chase it)* Aww. Bunny gone.

The Narrator-Dragons when young, were very small, very slow and as I said before; flightless.

Colin-Grass...grass...grass...*(Starts to eat grass)*

The Narrator-Young dragons ended up eating a lot of grass. Meanwhile, our beautiful and brave princess, along with the invaluable help of her mother's lady-in-waiting were scaling the mountains looking for scaly dragons. *(Nods and smiles as if saying yes I did say that)*

(Princess Madelina enters holding the sword awkwardly-perhaps by the tip and Daniela; the Queen's lady-in-waiting enters with a plastic container. A sign on the plastic container says gasoline)

Daniela-Oh Princess Madelina. Do slow down. It can't be good for your heart.

Princess Madelina-But soon it will be night. We must continue.

Daniela-Perhaps I could make it easier on you if I carried your sword.

Princess Madelina-It is not my sword dear Daniela. That is an error of grammar. I cannot claim what is not my own. In fact I think it is my mother the Queen's sword, though why she would have a sword is beyond me. She has never jousted before, and the only battles she has been involved in are domestic.

Daniela-May I carry the sword then? To lighten your burden.

Princess Madelina-Of course. Carrying a sword around, especially one that is not your own, can be a very tiresome business. *(Hands Daniela the sword)*

Daniela-Oh, before we encounter this fearsome beast, perhaps I can douse you with a flammable liquid like so. *(Douses her with imaginary gasoline)*

Princess Madelina-Oh my. What a horrid aroma. What is it?

Daniela-It is called gasoline. It's what causes the dragon's fire to ignite. I am sure the dragon will think you are only another dragon and thus you can sneak up in close proximity and deal the beast a death blow.

Princess Madelina-You are wise in the ways of dispatching beasts.

Daniela-I practiced on my own family.

Princess Madelina-What luck for me. So let's examine our preparations for battle. You have the sword.

Daniela-Check.

Princess Madelina-I am wearing the whatchma call it.

Daniela-Gasoline.

Princess Madelina-Gasoline. Is their anything else I would need?

Daniela-*(Takes out a blindfold)*

One Act Plays for Kids

Princess Madelina-What is that?

Daniela-The blindfold of invisiblity, so that the dragon won't be able to see you and you won't have to look at that ferocious creature.

Princess Madelina-I have read in a book that dragons are fearsome looking creatures.

Daniela-*(Ties the blindfold around Princess Madelina's eyes)* Can you see anything?

Princess Madelina-Nope, nothing.

Daniela-*(To audience)* Now, she has no way out. She will be burned by the dragon, fall off the mountain, or run into my sword, all of her own doing. You know if I weren't so common, I could be queen. *(laughs evilly as Colin the dragon approaches)* And here comes the ferocious fire-breathing dragon. I can't see how she is going to get out of this one. Now, I have one more trick up my sleeve. *(Grabs Princess and spins her)*

Princess Madelina-Oh my. What is happening to me? I am feeling very dizzy.

Daniela-It is the wind your highness. Please be careful. You might fall off the mountain.

Princess Madelina-*(Staggers around dizzily and puts her foot out)*

Daniela-There she goes! Over the edge!

Princess Madelina-*(Suddenly spins the other way)*

Daniela-Or not.

(Daniela, Princess Madelina and Colin freeze/slow down in their movements so as not to distract the audience from the next scene)

The Narrator-Meanwhile; as Princess Madelina was being disposed of in the mountains, Queen Anika and the Grand Vizier were cooking up a plot to kill the king.

Queen Anika-The strawberry muffins have been cooked, and so is the king's goose.

King Hector-Oh I like muffins, Mmmm-especially strawberry ones. But I didn't know I had a goose. What's his name?

Queen Anika-*(Looking at King Hector as if he was the dumbest thing on two feet)* What?

King Hector-My goose. It must have a name.

Queen Anika-Shut up you prattling fool!

King Hector-Shut up you prattling fool? I like it! Geese so often have boring monosyllabic names, like Doug, Fred, or Wendy. Shut up you prattling fool has an air of nobility about it, don't you think?

Queen Anika-*(To The Grand Vizier)* Quick! The poison!

The Grand Vizier-*(Lifts up a big jug of poison and empties the imaginary poison on the muffins)* There! That ought to do it!

Queen Anika-Where did you get all that poison, Vizier?

The Grand Vizier-Must I remind you that it is Grand Vizier. Grand!

Queen Anika-Of course. My apologies. Oh King Hector dear!

King Hector-Yes my loving queen?

Queen Anika-Would you like some strawberry muffins? They are so tasty good.

King Hector.-Why thank you wife! *(The Queen hands the plate of muffins to King Hector who consumes one or two in a frenzy)*

Queen Anika/The Grand Vizier-*(watch him intently)*

Queen Anika-Have another.

15

King Hector-They taste funny. *(Laughs suddenly and stops)*

The Grand Vizier-How are you feeling your majesty?

Queen Anika-Yes, any discomfort?

King Hector-*(Pats his stomach)* I feel fit as a fiddle.

The Grand Vizier-*(Grabs the Queen and leads her away from King Hector)* This is impossible. There was enough poison to kill fifty people!

Queen Anika-He has such a sweet tooth. He eats nothing but junk food, Perhaps he has built up a tolerance for poisons. After all, the food industry has been trying to kill us for years..

The Grand Vizier-Where's the royal sword? Perhaps we can cut off his head!

Queen Anika-No! I gave it to my trusty lady-in-waiting; Daniela, so she can get rid of Princess Madelina! I hope she is having better luck than we.

King Hector-May I have another strawberry muffin?

(Back to the three on the mountain top as King Hector, Queen Anika and the Grand Vizier freeze or move in slow motion. As before they must act in a non-distracting

manner and make no noise so that the audience will not become distracted when action focuses on the mountain scene)

Colin-*(Approaches Princess Madelina)* Mommy? *(Sniffs air)* Mmmmm. Gasoline! *(Fake licks gasoline off Princess Madelina then looks at Daniela)* Food! *(Attacks Daniela)* Food!

Daniela-*(Screams and tries to fight off Colin with the sword, but the sword falls)* Oh, no! I lost the sword! I am done for!

Princess Madelina- Daniela? *(She takes off her blindfold)* Daniela! Don't worry I will save you! Bad dragon!

Colin-*(Looks up sadly)* Bad dragon?

Princess Madelina-Don't eat my friend!

Colin-Friend?

Princess Madelina-*(Puts her arm around Daniela)* Yes... friend.

Colin-Can I be your friend?

Princess Madelina-Uh, sure. I guess. If you stop eating the humans.

Colin-OK. I eat grass. *(Starts eating grass)*

Daniela-Thank you for saving my life princess.

Princess Madelina-Well, what are friends for?

Colin-*(Looks up)* Friends?

Daniela-I wasn't a very good friend. I tried all sorts of ways to kill you.

Princess Madelina-You did? But why? Why would you want to kill me? Aren't I nice?

Daniela-Yes, you are very sweet, but palace politics, duplicitous plots, blind ambition, that sort of thing can get in the way of niceness and sweetness. And friendship.

Princess Madelina-Well I forgive you Daniela for trying to kill me, and you too Dragon for trying to eat my friend.

Colin- My name is Colin.

Princess Madelina-Colin is a very nice name for a dragon. My name is Princess Madelina and this is Daniela. Goodbye! *(They start to leave and Colin the dragon looks very sad)* Oh, do you want to come with us?

Colin- *(Smiles)* Colin has friends. *(Hurries after Princess Madelina and Daniela as they exit)*

The Grand Vizier-Meanwhile, down below, our murderous plans were not going so well.

King Hector-May I have another?

Queen Anika-Yee Gads! He'll have strawberries coming out of his ears!

The Grand Vizier-He just won't die!

(There is a commotion)

King Hector-I hear a commotion! What is the cause?

The Grand Vizier-*(Looks out imaginary window)*

Voices-Long live Queen Maddelina! Long live Queen Maddelina!

The Grand Vizier-Drat! Princess Maddelina is leading a procession of the people! And they are throwing confetti! How could they afford confetti? And our duplicitous lady-in-waiting is with her. And...

Queen Anika-And?

King Hector-And?

The Grand Vizier-She has captured a dragon!

Queen Anika-She who captures a dragon shall be queen. It is written in the ancient scrolls. She is the chosen one!

King Hector-A dragon? That's wonderful! The people love us again!

Charles Robertson

The Grand Vizier-Well, they love her at any rate.

(Musical overture as Princess Madelina enters followed by Daniela and Colin. Queen Anika, The Grand Vizier and King Hector all bow to Princess Madelina)

Queen Anika-I lie prostrate here and apologize with all my heart for trying to have you killed.

Princess Madelina-That's okay mother. Wait! You tried to have me killed?

Queen Anika-Yes, but I am sorry, so that's what counts, right?

Princess Madelina-Right. And this is the dragon Colin.

Colin-Food?

Princess Madelina-No, Colin, Remember you only eat the bad people.

Colin-*(Approaches The Grand Vizier)* Food?

The Grand Vizier- Please don't eat me! I am sorry that I tried by evil means to have the princess and the king killed. Please forgive me.

King Hector-*(Gets up)* You tried to kill me? *(The King points to the ground)*.

The Grand Vizier-*(falls prostrate)* Forgive me again.

King Hector-Princess Madelina, I am so pleased with your bravery, honesty, and sense of justice that I have decided to make you Queen! Queen of all the land!

Everybody-Yay!

Queen Anika-*(Takes off her crown and places it on Princess Madelina's head)* I am not worthy to be Queen, but you are; Queen Madelina!

Everybody-Yay!

King Hector-And furthermore, I think the Grand Vizier should be demoted to Lesser Vizier!

Everybody-Yay!

King Hector-And I shall retire from being a king to a life of leisure. *(Lies down in the second biggest throne)*

Princess Madelina-We all learned a lesson that we should not do mean things to people and forgive others when they say sorry.

Everybody-Yay!

Princess Madelina-I love happy endings.

King Hector-Did you know that I have a pet goose? Maybe Colin here, could play with it.

Colin-Food?

Princess Madelina-No Colin. Don't eat friends, even though they might taste good. Father; what is the goose's name.

King Hector-Shut up you prattling fool! *(Queen Madelina looks shocked)* Anybody want a strawberry muffin?

Queen Anika/The Grand Vizier-*(Run to prevent anyone from eating the muffins)* No! *(Everybody freezes)*

The Narrator-So, most people lived happily ever after in the land of Wobaggoneestoppeeland.

(Queen Madelina comes to the big throne and sits followed by her attentive ladies-in-waiting, Daniela and Anika-The Lesser Vizier kneels down to be a foot stool for Queen Madelina. The King sits in the medium-sized throne and Colin sits in the smallest chair)

Colin-Home.

The End

One Act Plays for Kids

GUPPY GETAWAY

By

Charles Robertson

Charles Robertson
GUPPY GETAWAY

An underwater fantasy about life under the sea for a school of guppies who get lost in the ocean

Characters

Humans
Father
Son

Guppies
Mother Fish
Fin
Gill
Minnie
Goldie
Angel
Flipper

Other Sea Creatures
Oscar
Sammy
Shark
Sea Cucumber
Shelby
Starfish
Sea Turtle
Electric Eel

Mermaids
Allegra
Aqua
Ariel

One Act Plays for Kids
GUPPY GETAWAY

(There is a riser or raised platform upstage-or in other words towards the back of the stage furthest from the audience-Downstage-or closer to the audience the stage is bare. The raised platform or riser will represent the land. The bare downstage area will represent the water. It can be decorated to represent an underwater world)

FATHER-*(Enters with SON on the platform with fishing gear-Can be fishing poles but there should be no fishing line or hooks)* Well, my boy...There it is. Lake Ontario. The history books, they say Ontario means sparkling water, H20, Aqua Vita. Now your mom says that fishing in Lake Ontario is like fishing in a sewer. You know what I say son?

SON-What Dad?

FATHER-I say your mom is a worry wart. Smell that air son. Are you smelling it?

SON-I'm smelling it dad.

FATHER-Nothing like it.

SON-Can I catch a shark dad?

FATHER-Well son , no. Sharks don't go for worms, or shiny lures.

Charles Robertson

SON-What do they go for dad? Huh? What do they go for?

FATHER-Actually boy...They might go for you, or maybe your little sister.

SON-Can I go get her.

FATHER-No son, I don't think that would be such a good idea. Your mom; she would get pretty riled up, and you know how your mom can be. Love her to death. She's a good woman and all, but she sure can get riled up.

SON-How's your face dad?

FATHER- *(Rubbing his cheek)* Still a little sore, son. I can't lie to you. But enough about me...Where was I?

SON-At the lake?

FATHER-I do not understand how you could have failed the fourth grade. Smart boy like you.

SON-They were against me dad; you know how them teachers can be.

FATHER-Yes I do....Now what you have to do is attach the lure to this hook see. *(Trying clumsily to attach the lure)* Ow...Ow...there. Attached! Success! Then we toss the line out so. *(Does so)* Now your turn...C'mon son. Don't be afraid.

SON-Could you do it dad? My fine motor skills being what they are and all.

FATHER-Sure son...*(He clumsily tries to attach the lure)* Ow...Ow...There! Now here you go boy. Now toss that line out carefully...

SON-Okay. *(He reaches back his pole and tosses out his imaginary line)*

FATHER- *(Winces)* Son I believe you have caught my ear.

SON-Oh sorry dad.

FATHER-Would you mind removing it please?

SON-Oh sure dad. *(Starts twisting the imaginary hook to get it out of his father's ear)*

FATHER-Ow...OOOwww!

SON-There! *(Holding the imaginary hook up in triumph)*

FATHER-Now toss your line out...gently.

SON-*(Tosses out his line)*

FATHER-There that's good.

SON-*(After a pause)* Now, what do we do?

FATHER-We wait.

SON-Wait for what?

FATHER-We wait for our fish, our Icthyosaurus, leviathan, guppy...Whatever grabs a hold of that hook, you better be ready to battle.

SON-And do we get to eat it dad?

FATHER-Well, son, that depends on how many eyes it has. You don't want to eat anything with more eyes in its head than you do. And if it glows in the dark, well, that's a good sign we're near some radioactivity. And if we're near some radioactivity, then I think we better just check ourselves into the nearest hospital.

SON-Okay dad. *(Beat)* This seems kinda boring...Is this boring?

FATHER-Well, son, its not just about the fishing, its about men bonding together.

SON-But I'm only in grade four.

FATHER-Someday, you will be a man, and you'll look back on this day and think...with a tear in your eye, that this was the best day of your life.

SON-If this is gonna be the best day of my life, I think I'm gonna have problems.

FATHER-This is where I get to tell my stories, spin my yarns, shoot the breeze.

SON-I've heard all your stories.

FATHER-Shush, boy. Just lie back, close your eyes, and listen to the waves.

FIN-*(Enters downstage) (He is examining his surroundings. He comes to the front of the audience and stares at them for a few seconds)*

MOTHER FISH-*(Entering)* Fin, you'll be late for school. Here's your lunch.

FIN-*(Stares at audience)*

MOTHER FISH-Fin!

FIN-What is it?

MOTHER FISH-What is what?

FIN-What's for lunch?

MOTHER FISH-Plankton.

FIN-But we always have plankton.

MOTHER FISH-Yes we do. Have a nice day.

FIN-I have a stomach ache.

MOTHER FISH-I am sure you do. Now get going.

GILL-*(Entering)* Is Fin ready?

MOTHER FISH-Yes he is.

FIN-No, I am not!

MOTHER FISH-Don't worry, I am sure things will go swimmingly.

GILL-They always do. Now come on Fin!.

FIN-Grumble grumble, grumble.

MOTHER FISH-And no grumbling. Remember, compared to other species, our brains are quite small. Life is quite complex and, well, usually our particular brand of fish is just not up to it, so learn all you can. It's a jungle out there, so to speak...Oh, and remember...

GILL-I know mom. Watch out for the big bad shark. Bye mom!

MOTHER FISH-Fin? *(Holds out her arms to hug Fin)*

FIN-Bye mom! *(He quickly hugs her as if to get it over with)*

MOTHER FISH-*(Exits)*

One Act Plays for Kids

GILL-*(Stands waiting with her little brother when after a few seconds the rest of the fish arrive-A school of guppies)*

MISS FLOUNDER-Hullo Gill. Hullo Fin. How are you today?

GILL & FIN- *(Without enthusiasm)* Hello Miss Flounder.

MISS FLOUNDER-I realize I am not of your species but that is quite alright. Quite as it should be.

MINNIE-Quite as it should be?

MISS FLOUNDER-I am an old fish and have learned many, many things.

MINNIE-What sorts of things?

MISS FLOUNDER-One of the key things that fish scientists have learned....

GOLDIE-Fish scientists?

MISS FLOUNDER-Sure. Most of us have not the brain capacity to become scientists but a few of us...we...what was I talking about?

GOLDIE-Brain capacity.

MISS FLOUNDER-Well, follow me.

FIN-Why are we going so slowly? Can't we go faster?

Charles Robertson

MISS FLOUNDER-I am a flounder, a solitary species that lives at the bottom of the ocean. I am actually quite out of my depth as a teacher of guppies. But who am I to question?

ANGEL-Excuse me.

MISS FLOUNDER-Yes?

ANGEL-What happened to Miss Tail Fin? She was nice.

MISS FLOUNDER-She got called up.

ANGEL-Called up?

MISS FLOUNDER-Yes, up there, way up there, well that's a beautiful world, and if you're lucky, you'll get called up.

ANGEL-I don't understand.

MISS FLOUNDER-Of course you don't dear. You are only a guppy.

GILL-Excuse me! Teacher!

MISS FLOUNDER-Yes?

GILL-Have you ever seen the big bad shark?

MISS FLOUNDER-Well, most of them have been called up, but there are still a few left, so you have to be careful. Its important not to stray.

FIN-Do they have big teeth?

MISS FLOUNDER-Huge teeth.

GOLDIE-Would they eat guppies?

MISS FLOUNDER-Only by accident.

FLIPPER-How can you accidentally eat someone?

ANGEL-I acci...dentally ate some flotsam once.

MISS FLOUNDER-Okay, we are coming to a turn...
Everybody....Oh look....Something shiny. I think I will eat
it. *(It is an imaginary shiny object)*

FLIPPER-Is that edible?

MISS FLOUNDER-I don't know. But it is shiny. *(She gulps it
and then jerks forward and then offstage)*

GOLDIE-*(Looking up)* Well, that was a surprise.

FIN-Where's the teacher?

ANGEL-I guess she just got called up. Lucky thing.

MINNIE-Now what do we do?

ANGEL-What's that? *(Pointing off stage)*

OSCAR-*(Enters limping)* Hello, little fishes. I am Oscar, the last King of the Octopuses. A solitary creature, I inhabit the ocean floor.

GILL-Why do you have so many legs?

OSCAR-Because, like I said, I am an octopus, I have one, two, three...uh, one two...I have many legs, uh, yes...Eight! I remember now. Eight! I have eight legs! Eight legs which I use to wrap my prey in.

SAMMY-But you only have seven.

OSCAR-Yes, How observant of you my friend. That's why the limp. An unfortunate incident with the big bad shark

MINNIE-Octopus? *(Laughs)* That's a funny name. What does it mean? Octopus?

OSCAR-Octo...pus? I think it is Greek for...eight legged cat. Yes! Many years ago, in the lost eons of time it is thought in our history, that we were distant relatives of the common house cat; mortal enemies of the gold fish.

FISH-Ooooh!

FLIPPER-What's a house cat?

OSCAR-Nasty, ugly, hairy creatures made up of teeth and claws that ended up somehow in the ocean. They went

34

through what my friend; Darwin the dog fish called evolution. They lost their hair, their teeth and claws and gained four legs and became the beautiful creature that you see before you now; the majestic octopus, denizen of the deep

FIN-What's this? *(Touching a sucker on the octopus)*

OSCAR-A suction cup which sticks to its prey….like so… *(Slowly pulls Fin in)* And then slowly I draw my prey to my mouth…Very slowly because that is how I do things….Slowly. Everything these days is so rush, rush, rush. I believe that one has to take his time, to enjoy his meal. Don't you agree little fish. I mean so many of us, we just cram our food down our mouths, but this is an occasion for celebration, to savour what we eat…

GILL-What we eat? Hey wait a minute, I may not be the smartest fish in the see but I see what's going on here. Is it lunch time?

OSCAR-Yes, yes indeed lunch time. Gather around, It is lunch time and guess what is on the menu for today.

SHARK-*(Entering)* Octopie!

OSCAR-*(Startled)* Who's that?

SHARK-C'mon Oscar, we have unfinished business.

35

OSCAR-Oh no! It's the big bad shark! Swim for your lives!

SHARK-Oh, come on, Oscar, I'm not that bad. Look at my nice shiny teeth. How can someone be bad when they have such nice shiny teeth? I am a tragic victim of my desires, my desire to eat octopie.

OSCAR-Isn't there someone else you'd rather eat?

SHARK-Let me think about that for a second...Actually no. Come here Oscar. Why do you run?

OSCAR-Force of habit.

SHARK-You wouldn't like me to starve would you?

OSCAR-Yes! Yes I would! I must release my secret weapon, my cloud of inky darkness. Like so. *(Escapes)*

SHARK-I can't see. *(Looks around)* Oscar! Come back! *(Exits)*

GILL-That was interesting

FIN-What about lunch?

GOLDIE-*(Sees SEA CUCUMBER lying on the floor. The Sea Cucumber can start the play by lying down in his or her spot)* Look at this. *(Pokes the sea cucumber)*

SEA CUCUMBER-*(Sits up)* Hello, I am a sea cucumber...
(Lies back down...Sits back up) That is all. *(Lies back down)*

GOLDIE-*(Pokes her again)*

SEA CUCUMBER-*(Sits up)* Hello, I am a sea cucumber...
(Lies back down and then sits up again) That is all. *(Lies back down)*

GOLDIE-*(Pokes SEA CUCUMBER again)*

SEA CUCUMBER-*(Sits up)* Enough already. You're bothering me. *(Lies back down)*

SHELBY-*(Enters)* Good evening ladies and gentlemen, and welcome to tonight's show. I am your host for the evening; Shelby the Shellfish. All you allergics stay back. How bout that water huh? Boy, is it wet or what? Oh look we have a school of minnows here.

SAMMY-Guppies.

SHELBY-Oh a heckler I'll keep my eye on you. Anyway, as I was saying. A shark goes to a restaurant and the maitre'd says to the shark; what brings you here and the shark says, I had nothing better to do. I just came just for the halibut...*(Guppies don't respond)* What are you? Sea cucumbers?

SEA CUCUMBER-*(Sits up)* Hello, I am a sea cucumber... *(Lies back down and then sits up)* That is all. *(Lies back down)*

SHELBY-Okay, stop me if you've heard this one before. A little mermaid was swimming through the rapidly depleting ecosystem that is the ocean. She stopped in front of a pretty sea anemone. Are you my anemone? she asked. No, replied the anemone. Mankind is your anemone....C'mon, please, some sign of life. What about that global warming huh?

SAMMY-Get off the stage!

SHELBY-What? Do you think its easy getting up in front of an audience with a repertoire of lame material and bad jokes. I mean, I'm not the writer. Why blame me? Oh well, I spose its not your fault that I'm a bad comedian, that I'm not funny.

FISH-*(Feeling sorry for Shelby)* Awww.

SHELBY-Its okay, *(Wiping his eyes)* I'll be alright. I just need a...moment.

STARFISH-*(Peeking out from backstage)* C'mon, I don't have all day!

SHELBY-Oh sure...Right away. Now performing! You've read about her...

MINNIE-I can't read.

SHELBY -You've heard about her! The one and only Miss Star Fish!

(Sound of dance music)

STARFISH-*(Does a simple dance step)* Star Fish, Sun fish. Gold fish, Blue Fish.

OSCAR-*(Limps on stage)* Swim for your lives!

STARFISH-Wait, didn't he used to have seven legs?

SHARK-*(Enters smiling toothily)* Come back here my pretty. We haven't finished lunch!

OSCAR-I'm shooting ink at you! I'm blinding you with ink!

STARFISH-Y'know, I never have to worry about losing my legs, I just regenerate.

SHELBY-Is that because you're a simple-minded creature?

STARFISH-Simple-celled you moron... So where you kids from?

ANGEL-We're lost and we don't know our way home...

(The Guppies cry)

Charles Robertson

STARFISH-*(Looking sincere)* Yes, well I am sure I care. Maybe we could do lunch. Are you edible? You're looking good, no really. Now do you want an autograph, or not?... I am very busy you know. I'm playing Atlantis next week. I have five arms. No waiting...*(There is no response from the guppies)* You wouldn't know real talent if ...what's the use.

SHELBY-Don't mind her. So, where you kids off to?

GILL-What's going to happen to Oscar?

SHELBY-Pretty much what happened to my career.

STARFISH-Shelby...Come on.

SHELBY-Uh, I have to go.

SAMMY-We're lost and...

SHELBY-I'm sure you are kid, but I gotta go...Bye. *(Starfish and Shelby exit)*

SAMMY-Now, what do we do?

MINNIE-Are we going to be lost forever?

SEA TURTLE-*(Enters slowly and sighs)*

GILL-Hello.

SEA TURTLE-Oh hello.

GILL-What are you?

SEA TURTLE-Isn't it obvious?

MINNIE-We're guppies. We have tiny brains. Nothing is obvious.

SEA TURTLE-I'm a sea turtle.

FLIPPER-Sea turtle, huh? Where do you live?

SEA TURTLE-Here. I live here. See. I always carry my house on my back.

GILL-That's convenient. We're lost. Do you know where our home is?

SEA TURTLE-No. But why don't you come with me? I could use the company. It will be nice to have someone to talk to. I am a rare and endangered species, so that means I can swim for thousands and thousands of miles and never meet another sea turtle. *(Sighs)* It gets rather lonely.

ALLEGRA-*(Entering with other mermaids)* So I says to him; If you can't remember my birthday, then, I don't need you. There are plenty of other fish in the sea.

AQUA-Not so much as there used to be.

ARIEL-Oh look, its one of those, uh...what is it?

41

SEA TURTLE-I am a sea turtle.

ALLEGRA-Oh yes. Sea turtle.

SEA TURTLE-You're so pretty. Would you be my friend?

AQUA-With a sea turtle? *(The Mermaids laugh)* I don't think so!

SEA TURTLE-But I'm a nice sea turtle. And I don't have any friends.

ARIEL-No wonder; Mobile Home girl. Oh look at the cute little guppies. Lets eat them.

SEA TURTLE-No, I won't let you eat my friends.

AQUA-What are you going to do about it?

SEA TURTLE-Withdraw my arms and legs and head into my shell.

ALLEGRA-And?

SEA TURTLE-And what?

AQUA-How does that stop us eating your friends?

SEA TURTLE-I don't know. I have a pretty rigid defensive posture.

ALLEGRA-Such a quaint thing.

AQUA-*(Waving a recipe)* Lets take this turtle home and make some soup. *(Drops the recipe on the ground)*

SEA TURTLE-Oh, I like soup.

ALLEGRA-Come with us then.

SEA TURTLE-Did you know that I am unique, a rarity among sea creatures in that I breathe air.

ARIEL-How disgusting! First you carry a house on your back and you breathe air. How socially uncool!

SEA TURTLE-It's a living

AQUA-Not for long. Let's go.

SEA TURTLE-I'm coming. *(Slowly moving after the mermaids)*

ALLEGRA-Hurry up you are so slow.

SEA TURTLE-I am a turtle you know...This is such fun. I've never had real friends before...

ANGEL-But what about us?

GILL-Yeah, aren't we your friends? *(Acts cute)*

SEA TURTLE-Not anymore. I'm with the cool people now. You'd cramp my style, so if you don't mind...Get lost!

SAMMY-But we're already lost.

ALLEGRA-Come on slow poke.

SEA TURTLE-Gotta go...

(The mermaids lead the sea turtle off stage)

GOLDIE-Come back sea turtle! Come back!

FLIPPER-*(Picking up a recipe that has been left by Aqua)* What's this?

MINNIE-What's what?

GILL-*(Taking the recipe from Flipper)* Oh, this is a recipe for turtle soup....*(They all nod)* TURTLE SOUP! Those mean mermaids are going to eat sea turtle girl! We have to rescue her!

SAMMY-Do we have to?

GILL-Yes, what's the worst thing that can happen to us?

SAMMY-We get eaten.

GILL-Besides that.

ANGEL-*(Puts up her hand)* We rescue the turtle?

GILL-Right. Let's rescue Turtle girl!

44

One Act Plays for Kids

(Other guppies grumble)

GILL-And no grumbling.

OSCAR-*(Entering)* For the love of Neptune...Leave me alone.

SHARK-*(Following Oscar on)* I would like to, really I would, but if I did let you go, I wouldn't be doing my job. You see I am a predator of the sea. I eat things. Even rubbery things like you. If I let you go, then where would I be?

OSCAR-I'm a predator, too.

SHARK-No, you're not. You're an entrée

OSCAR-*(Points off stage)* Oh look. A squirrel! *(Limps off in the opposite direction)*

SHARK- *(Looks in the direction that Oscar pointed)* What is a squirrel? *(Turns and sees that Oscar has fled)* Hey Oscar! Wait for me! *(Exits after Oscar)*

GOLDIE-Didn't he used to have six legs?

GILL-Come on guys...The rescue?

MINNIE-Oh yes, the rescue. I'd rather not.

(The guppies sit down in protest)

GILL-What kind of guppies are you?

FLIPPER-Live ones?

GILL-Well, then I'll have to go alone. *(Starts to exit and stops and looks back at the other guppies)* Guys?

FIN-*(Standing up)* Oh all right.

(The other guppies slowly get up and follow GILL off stage)

SEA TURTLE-*(Entering)* This is a nice place you got here.

ARIEL-*(Following the sea turtle on with the other mermaids. They are dragging on a big pot. The pot can be a small painted flat representing a pot. Should be light to carry)* You like it? Mind getting in this pot?

SEA TURTLE-Why?

ALLEGRA-All the cool girls are doing it now.

SEA TURTLE-Really? Alright then. *(She gets behind the pot. To the audience it should look as if she is in the pot)*

ALLEGRA-*(Starts sprinkling seasoning on the sea turtle)*

SEA TURTLE-*(Sneezes)* What are you doing?

ALLEGRA-Seasoning you.

ARIEL-The last turtle we had here was not seasoned properly.

AQUA-Now that was not my fault!

SEA TURTLE-*(Sneezes)*

AQUA-You know turtle girl, I think I'm going to like you. I think you have...taste.

SEA TURTLE-When I was little, my mother gathered us around after we had hatched; my six hundred brothers and sisters, and she told us in her motherly way, that we had better scamper to the sea, as fast as we could. In retrospect, I realized that the reason I had six hundred brothers and sisters, was that only a few of us would make it to the sea and carry on the species, because as you know, I am rare and endangered and that's why I don't have any friends because there are so few of us left.

ALLEGRA-That's fascinating.

ARIEL-*(Starts adding sea vegetables to the pot)* Soon you won't be lonely anymore-*(Laughs)*

SEA TURTLE-*(Laughs nervously)* What are you doing?

ARIEL-Adding some vegetables. You can't have soup without vegetables.

SEA TURTLE-You're so thoughtful...in a culinary way. I like having friends. What kind of soup?

AQUA-Turtle soup!

MERMAIDS -*(Laugh and then SEA TURTLE joins them)*

SEA TURTLE-Wait a minute! That's not funny!

AQUA-Maybe not to you....

ALLEGRA-Remember, she has to simmer.

SEA TURTLE-I thought mermaids were supposed to be nice!

AQUA-Listen turtle girl. You should feel honoured. We're picky eaters. We don't just eat anything.

SEA TURTLE-Well, it's true. I do feel a little flattered. What am I saying? I'm leaving! *(Tries to get out of the pot)*

ALLEGRA-*(Pushes her back in)* You're not going anywhere. *(The mermaids and the sea turtle freeze)*

OSCAR-*(Rolling onstage)* Meanwhile, I was having problems of my own.

ELECTRIC EEL-*(Enters twitching and sees Oscar)* What are you?

SEA CUCUMBER-I am a sea cucumber...That is all.

ELECTRIC EEL-No, not you...You. *(Pointing at Oscar)*

OSCAR-I am the legendary octopus. Denizen of the deep.

ELECTRIC EEL-Aren't you supposed to have a multitudinous quantity of legs?

OSCAR-Usually. Usually. But well, it was the big bad shark.

ELECTRIC EEL-Yes? *(Twitches)*

OSCAR-What's wrong with you? In fact, what are you?

ELECTRIC EEL-I'm *(Twitches)* Edward; The Electric Eel and I have this uncontrollable twitch, this short circuit. My wires are scrambled.

OSCAR-Well, normally I would care, but I have bigger fish to fry, so to speak.

ELECTRIC EEL-Can I help?

OSCAR-What are you again?

SEA CUCUMBER-*(Sits up)* I am a sea cucumber...That is all.

OSCAR-You can be very annoying.

ELECTRIC EEL-I am an eel, a slick graceful *(Twitches)* creature of the deep. At least I'm supposed to be. But as an eel, I am not so slick. *(Twitches)* I have no friends. I am supposed to have an electrifying personality, a spark, but...*(Twitches)* I am handicapped by this twitch. People stare at me all the time.

OSCAR-Join the club. I have as many friends as I have legs.

SEA CUCUMBER-*(Sits up)* Can I be part of your gang?

ELECTRIC EEL-Are you not some sort of vegetable?-

SEA CUCUMBER-Some sort. I'm adrift in the evolutionary flow. I don't exactly know what I am. Half plant, half animal.

ELECTRIC EEL-Are you edible?

SEA CUCUMBER-Do you think its easy to have friends when you are stuck to the ocean floor? I am a sea cucumber. Tis true, but I am so much more. I have thoughts and dreams like any other creature that swims or floats in the sea kingdom.

ELECTRIC EEL-Yes, but are you edible?

SEA CUCUMBER-Uh...No.

OSCAR-Oh, oh. It's the big bad shark.

ELECTRIC EEL-Let's freeze. Maybe it won't see us.

(They freeze)

One Act Plays for Kids

SHARK-*(Entering)* Hullo. Has anybody seen an octopus about? *(Exasperated)* Excuse me. I can see you.

ELECTRIC EEL-What does this octopus look like?

SHARK-It has eight legs and is very stupid.

ELECTRIC EEL-I don't see anything like that around here.

SHARK-*(Looking down at Oscar and Sea Cucumber)* What are you?

SEA CUCUMBER/OSCAR-*(Sitting up)* I am a sea cucumber...That is all.

SHARK-*(Bending down to study Oscar)* Hmm. Something very familiar about you.

ELECTRIC EEL-Maybe he went that away. *(Suddenly points in the distance)*

SHARK-That away?

ELECTRIC EEL-Yep. That away.

SHARK-Fine, but if you're lying to me, I will be back and it will be an eel meal. Good day.*(Exits)*

OSCAR-Well, that was close. Thank you buddy.

ELECTRIC EEL-No problem. I don't like sharing my food.

OSCAR-What?

ELECTRIC EEL-I've been feeling a little peckish myself.

OSCAR-Peckish?

ELECTRIC EEL-Hungry.

OSCAR-And I am almost afraid to ask, but what by chance do you eat?

ELECTRIC EEL-Well. Lets put it this way...*(Twitches)* The cucumber is safe.

OSCAR-Oh no. *(Rolls off)*

ELECTRIC EEL-Come back here. *(Twitches)* Come back. I feel some sort of connection. *(Twitches and follows Oscar off stage)*

SEA CUCUMBER-*(Sits up)* You know, its very lonely here on the bottom of the ocean floor, but it also usually quiet, which in the hustle bustle of life can be quite relaxing... That is all. *(Lies back down)*

SEA TURTLE-*(The sea turtle and the mermaids unfreeze)* Help...Help....

ARIEL-Please be quiet and enjoy the meal.

FLIPPER-*(Entering with the other guppies)* There's sea turtle!

ANGEL-What shall we do?

FIN-Lets attack!

SAMMY-What?

GILL-He said; Let's attack! *(The guppies surround the mermaids)*

ALLEGRA-What's going on?

AQUA-We're being attacked by mad guppies.

ARIEL-They might have rabies...Swim! *(Mermaids exit)*

SEA TURTLE-Thank goodness, you arrived just in time. Help me out...*(The guppies help her out)* Thank you so much for rescuing me, and I am so sorry I said you guys were uncool.

GILL-That's okay. We can be friends now.

SEA TURTLE-I just wanted to be popular.

MINNIE-You can be popular with us.

SAMMY-Now what? We're still lost.

SEA TURTLE-Follow me. I know a gully where the guppies frolic. Follow me. I think I know how to get you back home. Follow me.

(The sea turtle leads the guppies in a brief slow motion swim-perhaps to music-Other than Gill and Fin the other guppies swim slowly offstage to the music leaving Gill, Fin and the Sea Turtle onstage)

MOTHER FISH-*(Enters)* Oh hello...You're back from school already.

GILL-Yes. Miss Flounder got called up, and then there was this octopus that kept getting eaten by a shark, and there was this starfish and she was beautiful...

FIN-And the mermaids...Don't forget the mermaids.

MOTHER FISH-What did Fin say?

GILL-There were these mermaids.

MOTHER FISH-*(Sees the sea turtle)* Oh hello. Who are you?

SEA TURTLE-I am a sea turtle. I have no friends.

GILL-Can she stay with us?

GILL & FIN- Pleeeaaaasee!

MOTHER FISH-Oh, how can I say no to such adorable little faces. Oh alright.

SEA TURTLE-Yay! I have a real family now! *(They exit)*

(Scene Change-Father and son on the platform are looking down at Miss Flounder)

MISS FLOUNDER-*(Lying on the ground gasping-A fish out of water)*

SON-Is that a shark dad?

FATHER-No son, I think you caught yourself a flounder.

SON-Flounder, huh? Can we eat it?

FATHER-I don't think so, son. Its been in the lake. You don't want to eat anything that's been in the lake.

SON-Then maybe we could keep it. We could keep it in the bathtub.

FATHER-No, I can't think that your mom would be too happy. No son. I think, I think we gotta let our scaly little friend go back into the poisonous waters from whence it came. *(Tries to push Miss Flounder back into the water)* Help me son.

SON-Yeah, sure dad.

Charles Robertson

FATHER-She's a big one. Too much muscle to be good eatin anyway. Okay son, push...

SON-Bye fish! *(They push Miss Flounder off the platform in a safe manner and she swims away off stage)*...Dad?

FATHER-Yes son.

SON-If we ain't gonna eat the fish, why do we fish?

FATHER-Its about bonding son. Its about family. Its about quality time. If we want to eat fish, your mother has to buy it at the grocery store.

SON- Can I tell mom about the fish that got away?

FATHER-Of course son. Of course. She is expecting it. Come on. *(They exit with the father's arm around his son's shoulder)*

The End

Night of the Gnomes

by

Charles Robertson

Charles Robertson

NIGHT OF THE GNOMES

Four garden gnomes rise up in rebellion against their human masters.

Characters

Narrator

The Norwegian Family

Thomas Verstag
Alexandra Verstag
Ilsa Verstag

The Gnomes

King Fijord
Doctor Djorksted
The Maestro
Fourth Gnome

The Tourists

Patricia
Mom
Aunt Julia

NIGHT OF THE GNOMES

(Lights up on a little house, which can be little more than a flat surrounded by shrubbery, trees and mushrooms. Everything should be very simple. 4 gnomes in various costumes stand frozen in the garden)

Narrator-For centuries gnomes have battled with humans. Humans have battled with gnomes. The battle of Mjorstad was a major turning point. Fought in the deep snow, the short gnomish legs could not function successfully in the Scandinavian winter elements. Assisted by the Gods of the North; Thor, Odin and Fria, the humans crushed the gnomish hordes. The surviving gnomes were taken to Asgard and imprisoned on the lawns and in the gardens of the Norse Gods and Demi-gods and placed under a spell. Though the gnomes were still technically alive, they were unable to move, their little hearts unable to beat, their blood; frozen in their veins. They could not move, even when knocked down by rampaging kids. Oh the humiliation of these once mighty short warriors! Odin soon tired of the gnomish remnants of this once great race. He told the mischievous Loki to take the gnomes and plant them in the gardens and lawns of the great civilizations of man, to stand forever guard, to scare away the crows, the pigeons and small vicious children. But our story does not end there. A peculiar family of gardeners had managed to secure four of these hideous garden gnomes. The head of the family had delved, yes that's the word I'm using, delved into the Scandinavian myths, and he knew a day of reckoning was at hand. He knew the day of nomenclature was at hand, the day that gnomes would finally get back their names and rebel against their human masters. One misunderstood man understood. His story.

(The Gnomes start marching in place and chanting)

Gnome Chant

We are gnomes great and small

We are gnomes great and small

We will join our brothers

and rise up!

Rise up trolls and elves and gnomes

Rise up and take human homes

Kill the humans!

Kill the humans!

We are gnomes great and small

We are gnomes great and small

One Act Plays for Kids
(The gnomes freeze)

Thomas-*(Enters)* I feel a reckoning coming on, a day that the earth will remember. Yes sir; you know it. I'm talking about gnomes. Folks round here may think I'm crazy, not playing with a full deck, cognitively impaired. They call me Thomas Verstag; the Norwegian nutbar, the Scandinavian psycho. But I've ciphered through my books. Done some internet investigation. I have read my tea leaves, searched the stars at night and called on roadside fortune tellers. All the signs point to a coming resurrection, a coming Ragnorok. where the old gods will be replaced by these little fellers here, the fearsome and hideous gnome. *(He starts to talk to the gnomes)* Hey little fellers. What are you up to? Don't think I don't know what's going on in those little wooden heads of yours.

Alexandra-*(Enters)* Papa, who are you talking to, and why are you up so early?

Thomas-The night of the gnome is upon us.

Alexandra-But papa, these things aren't real. They are manufactured, by unskilled labour by the looks of things, but manufactured they are. Ever since mama took a vow of silence, you have, how should I put this delicately? Gone off the deep end.

Thomas-Shush daughter! Look at this! These gnomes have moved!

Alexandra-Oh papa.

Thomas-I suspected as much. Look! *(He crouches down beside the gnomes)* I put stones by their feet and the stones are here, *(Indicating a small distance)* and their feet are there. *(Holds out his hand)* Measuring tape!

Alexandra-Oh, papa, what is to become of us? We will be the laughing stock of Nordverk.

Thomas-The measuring tape if you don't mind. I will show you who has gone crazy and who is merely a genius.

Alexandra-Here. *(Hands him the measuring tape)*

Thomas-*(Measures the gnome's feet)*

Alexandra-Well?

Thomas-I knew it! 5 centimeters! They have transported themselves, each of them, by 5 centimeters. This is historic!

Alexandra-They'll be running marathons before long.

Thomas-*(Stands up)* I am afraid my dear child, that is not possible. The muscles stiffen up after so many centuries of non-use. They atrophy. Besides; gnomes were never known for their cardiovascular abilities. Note the short and powerful legs. Good for sprinting. They could bring down an antelope. An antelope I tell you! See this little guy here. Teeth like piano keys. Used to be known as the Maestro. See those incisors. Could take the flesh off your bones in seconds. See this sprightly feller. See the regalness?

Alexandra-They all look the same to me.

Thomas-Don't they teach you nuthin' at school! That's King Fijord, king of all gnomes.

Alexandra-King Fijord?

Thomas-He was the one that led the rebellion against the humans.

Alexandra-And you happen to have him right here?

Thomas-Yup. You can tell that he is a little bit smarter than the others.

Alexandra-Are these things capable of being smart?

Thomas-Who knows. What is clear is that they are capable of being quite vicious. It was taught to all the young Nordic folk. When battlin' a gnome, avoid their teeth at all costs. Well, I'm feeling a bit peckish. I wonder when breakfast will be ready. Wife!

63

Charles Robertson

Thomas' Wife Ilsa-*(Enters-Sees Thomas and Alexandra and makes an elaborate mime show about dinner)*

Alexandra-Oh Papa. Look! Mama is trying to say something to us. What's she sayin?

Thomas-Dagnabit; how should I know? I'm illiterate when it comes to the spoken language of the mime.

Alexandra-Something about singing in a microphone. And dancing I think.

Thomas-Let's indulge the dear lady and see what she's up to.

(The humans exit)

King Fijord-*(Lets out a breath)* I thought those sub humans would never leave.

Fourth Gnome-Can we do our song again? Huh? Can we? Can we?

King Fijord-No my ultra enthusiastic little minion. No songs for now. Doctor Djorksted?

Doctor Djorksted-Yes?

King Fijord-What are your plans for overthrowing the reign of the humans.

Doctor Djorksted-Well, its quite simple actually.

Fourth Gnome-Overthrowing the humans? But I would rather do the song. I like the song. Overthrowing the humans seems like a lot of work. There are only 4 of us. And there are, *(Starts counting on his fingers)* uh, many humans.

Doctor Djorksted-Over 7 billion. But there are thousands of us, spread across the world, standing silent guard over homes, lawns and gardens, battered by the elements but waiting, waiting for the call to action.

The Maestro-Doctor; I admire your enthusiasm, being outnumbered as we are by about a million to one. I too, had enthusiasm in my younger years. Remember my stirring song as we marched off to doom in our last battle? Gnomes from Alaska, from Denmark and Canada, from the United States of America, from Switzerland and France, from England and the Canary Islands and, well it just sort of went on and on. You get the picture..

Fourth Gnome-And nothing rhymed.

The Maestro-Of course it didn't rhyme. I'm an artiste. I don't rhyme.

Fourth Gnome-Well, it would have been easier to remember the song. One of us is singing France, and someone else is trying to sing Asia Minor, and another person is, well, we were so confused that when the humans attacked we weren't ready, fighting as we were about the words to that dumb song.

The Maestro-From field and fijord, little gnomes get out of bed and kill...

King Fijord-Stop your inane prattlings. The song was a mistake, however Doctor Djorsted has a plan.

Fourth Gnome-Is it better than our usual battle plan of raising our arms above our heads and hurling insults.

Doctor Djorksted-Much better. The simplicity of our victory will be achieved in their lack of belief. What happened to the Norse Gods?

Fourth Gnome-*(Puts up his hand)* They lost to science?

Doctor Djorksted-Yes my boy. They did indeed lose to science. It was scientifically proven to the Gods that they couldn't possibly exist so they did their part for science and stopped existing.

King Fijord-A very convenient turn of events for us.

Fourth Gnome-But are we not mythical creatures too? Could scientists not prove that we couldn't exist, that our being made of wood was incongruous with our having the ability to think?

Doctor Djorsted-No, because we are not smart enough to be so easily convinced. The humans however, bedevilled as they are by their science, will believe our existence; illogical, and thus we can take them by the element of surprise. We could be on prime time television, munching on humans flesh with our phenomenal teeth, and they still wouldn't believe their own eyes. In their minds, we can't exist and so to them we won't. And thus we will defeat them. Simple, huh?

Fourth Gnome-I don't know. I think if we're going to win this thing we need a song that rhymes, a song that the boys can remember.

The Maestro-Don't worry. I will write a better song.

King Fijord-Hush! Someone is coming!

(The gnomes assume their previous gnome-like positions)

Patricia-*(Enters)* Mom, this is so boring. I am only a child. Children can only deal with so much boredom before their heads explode.

Mom-*(Hurrying to catch up)* Now Patricia, darling, your Aunt Julia is enjoying our forced march through the homes and gardens of Nordverk, aren't you Aunt Julia?

Charles Robertson

Aunt Julia-*(Entering with a cup off coffee and a map under her arm)* What? Oh yes. You would think they could make a decent cup of coffee. How do these people manage to wake up without a good cup of coffee?

Mom-Aunt Julia! The map! Where are we?

Aunt Julia-Uh, oh yes. *(Putting the coffee down and opening up the map)* Where are we?

Mom-*(Sighs)* Nordverk.

Aunt Julia-Oh yes. *(Reading from the map)* Uh, this appears to be the home of Thomas Verstag. He is a champion grower of fungus.

Patrica-Wow! Look at the mushrooms. I bet their poisonous. Can I eat one?

Mom-Don't be silly dear. Your father would miss you.

Aunt Julia-What a fabulously dreary place. *(Picks up coffee)*

Mom-It's the ocean breeze. Keeps everything damp. Good for mushrooms.

Aunt Julia-*(Touching her hair)* Not good for my hair though.

One Act Plays for Kids

Patricia-Hey mom *(Running up to The Maestro and staring at him)* What's this?

Mom-Its a gnome.

Patricia-Looks like a dwarf or something.

Aunt Julia-Oh, I hate gnomes. They are one garden ornament I could do without. Why one would choose to decorate ones beautiful garden with these hideous creatures is beyond me.

Patricia-*(Tapping The Maestro on the head)* Must be made of wood or something. Look at them!

Aunt Julia-Yes, how could one not look at them. Frightful creatures.

Mom-*(Ignoring Patricia as she approaches Aunt Julia to peek over her shoulder at the map.)* Is there anything about them in the guide?

Aunt Julia-What? Oh...Yes. *(Putting coffee down and opening up the map again)* Legend has it that the gnomes led by King Fijord were defeated by the Gods and humans at the battle of Mjorstad.

(Meanwhile the gnomes grab Patricia and run off)

Mom-Hmm, interesting. What's next?

Aunt Julia-Nordic roses. The castle of Hans Vestvistle. *(Pointing off stage)* Its about a kilometer this way.

Mom-Hmm. Patricia. Lets go. Patricia?

Aunt Julia-*(Seeing that the gnomes are gone)* Where are the gnomes?

Mom-They're gone! Patricia! Put back the gnomes! You'll get us in a whole stack of trouble. I am sure it is against the law to steal gnomes.

Aunt Julia-It says here that gnomes are protected under the endangered species act of 1941.

Mom-Patricia!

Aunt Julia-You could go to jail!

Mom-Patricia!

Ilsa-*(Comes out of the house and starts gesturing)*

Aunt Julia-Ahh, she must be afflicted with mime syndrome. Its a chronic ailment found in clusters of rural Nordic communities.

Ilsa-*(More hand waving and gesturing)*

Mom- My daughter has run off with your gnomes and we must find her.

One Act Plays for Kids

Ilsa-*(More extravagant gesturing)*

Aunt Julia-I wonder what she's trying to say.

Mom-Something about flying a desk.

Aunt Julia-Perhaps there might be someone else we can talk to.

Ilsa-*(Turns and puts her hands to her mouth and mimes yelling)*

Aunt Julia-Yeah, as if that's going to work.

Mom-*(Grabs Aunt Julia by the arm and drags her to the house)* Come on. *(Knocks on the door of the house)*

Alexandra-*(Comes out from the house)* Papa! Papa! There's two fancy ladies wearin' perfume and such.

Thomas-*(Follows Alexandra out)* Hush child. Hello Ladies. What can I do for you? If you're from the tax department, I will be getting my gun.

Mom-I am afraid my daughter has stolen your garden gnomes.

Thomas-But each gnome weighs about 80 pounds!

Aunt Julia-Eighty pounds?

Thomas-How old is your daughter?

Charles Robertson

Mom-Ten.

Thomas-Oh darn those little fellers. Your daughter hasn't kidnapped my gnomes. They have kidnapped her! This is a very exciting development.

Mom-Exciting? What exactly do you mean?

Thomas-Don't you see, this is the dawning of the night of the gnomes. Soon, garden gnomes everywhere will be attacking their human masters. You see, people didn't believe me. They thought I was some crazy old coot. But you see this proves I was right. That I'm not a coot. When we find the mangled body of your daughter, then the world will have to pay attention. Maybe the gnomes will appoint me their ambassador to Norway. I'm practically delirious with excitement.

Aunt Julia-But gnomes are made of wood or something, aren't they? Or plaster?

Thomas-But wood or plaster, the gnomes are plotting to overthrow the humans. There must be thousands of gnomes around the world. Imagine the terror they will unleash on humanity.

Mom-But can't you just kick them, knock them over, or something?

Thomas-Come with me everybody! We must find them! Your daughter won't have much time. Wife, come with us.

Ilsa-*(More extravagant miming)*

Aunt Julia-Is she deprived of speech?

Thomas-She has taken a vow of silence. It makes our philosophical discussions at the dinner table hard to follow. *(Bends down)* Look! Tiny footprints. The gnomes have skedaddled in this direction. Daughter; get me my gun. Lock yourself up in the family hut. If the gnomes come fer ya, call the gardening society of Norway. They'll know what to do.

Alexandra-But papa.

Thomas-No but papas. Get me the gun. *(Alexandra disappears imto the house)* Young uns. Always questioning authority and getting into the blueberries.

Alexandra-*(Returns with preferably an old musket and hands it to Thomas)*

Thomas-Thanks girl. Now lock yerself in the house

Alexandra-But papa. I'm scared.

Thomas-Silence girl. We got some gnomin' to do. *(To others)* Lets go!

73

Charles Robertson
Mom-My poor girl. I hope she's alright!

(They exit)

Alexandra-*(Watches them go and enters the house-
Perhaps the house flat can be taken off and a tree flat
brought on)*

*(The lights change and the gnomes enter with Patricia,
whose hands are tied behind her back)*

The Maestro-Meanwhile, we had arrived at a clearing in
the woods. We had tied the human's hands behind its
back and we were planning our next move.

King Fijord-This looks like a good spot. Let's rest for
awhile.

(The gnomes and Patricia sit)

Fourth Gnome-So what are we going to do with it?

Doctor Djorksted-Humans are our mortal enemies. We
have to extinguish them, each and every one of them
nasty creatures. Once we get rid of her, we only have uh,
something like; six billion, nine hundred and ninety-nine
million, nine hundred and ninety-nine thousand, nine
hundred and ninety-nine humans to go!

Fourth Gnome-*(Sighs)* That makes me tired just thinking about it.

Patricia-I think you should let me go.

King Fijord-And why is that?

Patricia-Because you can't win. There are too many of us.

King Fijord-There in lies our strength, the element of surprise. We are few in number but short in stature. The time of humans is coming to its predestined end and the night of the gnome is coming. Maestro! Lead us in a rousing chorus of kill the humans!

(The gnomes start singing)

Rise up trolls and elves and gnomes

Rise up and take human homes

The Maestro-Wait! Wait! Someone is not singing.

(They all look at Patricia)

Patricia-Who me? But I don't want to sing 'kill the humans'. I am a human.

The Maestro-There will be no exceptions. Now sing!

Patricia-Alright, but I won't be happy about it.

Charles Robertson
The Maestro-Please; everybody with feeling.

(As song goes along Patricia becomes more and more enthusiastic)

Rise up trolls and elves and gnomes

Rise up and take human homes

Kill the humans!

Kill the humans!

We are gnomes great and small

We are gnomes great and small

Patricia-That was fun. Inspirational actually.

The Maestro-Thank you. I consider it my best work.

Patricia-So why do you hate humans so much?

King Fijord-We once ruled the earth. An empire of little people. Cousins to elves and trolls, we frolicked in hill and dale. But then the humans came and infringed upon our woodland habitat.

Doctor Djorksted-We were driven deeper and deeper into the woods. We realized that if we didn't fight back, we would soon disappear from the earth, so King Fijord organized a great army. Must have been a thousand of us, along with our cousin elves and trolls. On the other side, the humans allied themselves with Thor, Odin and the other Norse Gods.

The Maestro-Well, despite my best efforts to stir my fellow gnomes' hearts with my music, we got bogged down in the snow.

Fourth Gnome-You see we have short legs and when the snow is deep our mobility is challenged.

King Fijord-It wasn't a fair fight.

Doctor Djorksted-But now our revenge is nigh.

The Maestro-We have been planning this moment for several millennium. And now the time has come.

Patricia-How are you gonna win? Do you have like magical powers? Could you turn my Aunt Julia into a toad?

Doctor Djorksted-Magic powers? No.

Patricia-Then what is your secret weapon?

Doctor Djorksted-Fellow gnomes. Unleash the full power of our gnashing!

(The gnomes raise their arms over their heads and shake their arms while mumbling incoherently)

Patricia-And that's it?

King Fijord-Terrifies our enemies.

The Maestro-Yes, its very fearsome isn't it?

Patricia-Actually its kind of cute.

Fourth Gnome-And we can gnaw at the humans with our teeth.

Patricia-Oh, you have sharp teeth? That's hopeful.

Doctor Djorksted-Well, our teeth are built for eating mushrooms and certain leaves and roots. See. *(Opens his mouth)*

Patricia-How disappointing. No fangs? How about claws?

King Fijord-No, we're just a less intelligent and less violent form of human.

Fourth Gnome-Doomed to the evolutionary garbage dump.

Patricia-Well maybe I can help you.

The Maestro-But you're human. You're our first prisoner.

Patricia-Set me free and I can help you. No, no. I will join you!

Doctor Djorksted-*(To the other gnomes)* I don't trust her. *(To Patricia)* You would join us? Why?

Patricia-Because otherwise I will have to go on these excruciatingly boring sight-seeing trips with my mom and aunt. Taking part in a war against humanity seems a little more exciting.

King Fijord-Shh! Someone is coming!

Doctor Djorksted *(Sniffs the air)* Humans!

King Fijord-Quick untie her. We will need all the help we can get. *(The gnomes untie her)*

King Fijord-Let's freeze, and then on my signal, attack.

All-*(Freeze including Patricia)*

Thomas-*(Entering)* This way.

Mom-Oh dear! It's my little girl. She's been turned into one of those horrid gnomes

King Fijord-*(Raises his arms above his head)* Attack! *(Looks around but none of the others have followed suit)* And again I say, Attack!

Gnomes-*(And Patricia raise their hands above their heads and yell)* Bjorgen, Mjorgen EEEEEEEEEE!

Thomas-Oh no! The gnomes are attacking!

Aunt Julia-What did they say?

Thomas-Loosely translated it means. You're stupid and you smell funny...EEEEEEEEEEEEEE!

Ilsa-Well, I'll be gob-smacked.

Thomas-Wife, have you dropped your anti-verbal ways?

Ilsa-Well, I couldn't sit quietly by for the whole play now could I? That would be silly. What do these creatures want?

Patricia-*(King Fijord is about to say something when Patricia interrupts him)* We gnomes have several grievances. *(Pulls out a long sheet of paper)*

Aunt Julia-Its the Stockholm Syndrome.

Mom-The what?

Aunt Julia-Never mind.

Mom-Patricia; you come here right now!

Patricia-No, not til our demands are met.

Doctor Djorksted-What demands? We have demands?

Ilsa-Well, I think we could work something out. We could set aside a little patch of ground for the gnomes in our garden and declare it the first principality of the Gnome.

Thomas-Now wife, I'm the thinker in this family. I yearn for your silent ways.

The Maestro-Principality. I like that. And I could create our first gnational anthem.

Ilsa-Think of the tourist dollars we will generate. We will, all of us, share in the wealth. People the world over have a strange fascination with gnomes. And Gnomes, the world over, will migrate here to their gnomeland. We will have a thriving industry. Maybe a theme park!

Patricia-Rides?

Ilsa-The biggest!

Fourth Gnome-And fungus. We like fungus. Can we have fungus?

Thomas-All the fungus you can eat. Wife, I am beginning to see what you mean.

Mom-*(Checking her watch)* Oh my. Look at the time. We have to be leaving. Patricia? Are you coming?

Patricia-I've done my part. Bye guys.

Gnomes-*(Looking sad)* Bye.

Patricia-Don't worry. I'll be back. I promise. Hey everybody! How about one more rousing chorus of Kill the Humans!

(Everybody sings)

Rise up trolls and elves and gnomes

Rise up and take human homes

Kill the humans!

Kill the humans!

We are gnomes great and small

We are gnomes great and small

The End

Toys in the Closet

by

Charles Robertson

Charles Robertson

TOYS IN THE CLOSET

Toys in the Closet speaks to the imagination in all children-The idea that their toys are alive

Characters

Narrator

Sisters
Molly
Her little sister Maggie

Toys
Fairy Godmother
Stuffed Dragon
Plastic Soldier
Happy Face the Clown
Baby Doll
Fashion conscious Doll
Porcelain Ballerina

Foster Family
Foster Sister
Foster Mother

TOYS IN THE CLOSET

(The set should consist of over-sized furniture and things one would find in a child's room including a toy box)

(There are seven dolls. A ballerina on a small rise, a soldier, a dragon, a fairy godmother, a fashion conscious doll, a clown and a baby doll)

(Under a top light, the dolls are pulled slowly to their feet as if by invisible strings. Their faces are passive; like, well, dolls)

(They freeze)

Narrator-*(Enters)* Once upon a time...Oh dear. That's not the way to start this story at all. I get so flustered when there are people listening to me. You see this is a fairy tale. And here's the Fairy Godmother, though she's not real. She is just a doll as are all these others. They are just dolls. Now of course the thing about dolls, the secret is, that they can become real through kids' imaginations. And here's the fierce dragon, though he doesn't have any blood or guts inside, just cotton or something. And here's the brave soldier who lost his arm in the toy box, and has been looking for it ever since. There's Happy Face the Clown. Pull his string and he laughs. And there's the

85

fashion doll. Everybody knows her. Oh, and see that little one there. That's baby doll. And this one here, this is the beautiful ballerina doll made of porcelain. She is up on a shelf so that she will not break. She gets very lonely up there. So do you see my problem? This story takes place right about now, so I can hardly say once upon a time now can I? Oh, wait! Where are they?

Maggie & Molly-*(Enter-When the dolls are moved by Molly and Maggie the children playing the dolls should move their limbs stiffly and their faces should remain passive-as doll-like as possible)*

Narrator-You see that little girl there? That's Molly. And that is her little sister Maggie. These are their dolls. They live with their mean foster parents and foster stepsister. (*Shrugs*) Hey it's a fairy tale. Somebody has to be mean.

Molly-*(Playing with Soldier Doll)* Aye aye sir! *(Molly raises the soldier's arm in a salute)*

Maggie-*(Starts moving the dragon forward)* Roar! Roar!

Molly-Oh, oh. Here comes the fierce dragon. He's breathing fire and everything!

Maggie-Roar! Roar!

Molly-Oh no! Its going to eat the dancing princess! Here comes Happy Face! I'll help you soldier boy! *(Molly moves*

Happy Face's arms up and down) Chop! Chop! *(Molly grabs Fashion Doll and makes the doll's leg go up)* Fashion Doll kicks the Fire-Breathing Dragon!

Maggie-*(Pulls the dragon backward)* Roar?

Molly-Then Baby Doll comes out! *(Pulls the doll's string)*

Baby Doll-*(Crawls forward)* Mama, mama.

Maggie-*(Grabs Baby Doll and gives it to the Dragon)(Evil Laugh)*

Molly-The Dragon steals Baby Doll and is about to burn her face off when...*(Molly moves the Fairy Godmother forward and lifts up her wand arm)* The Baby's Fairy Godmother flies up on her wings and puts a spell on the terrible ferocious dragon and turns him into a...salamander! The end!

Maggie-What's a salamander?

Narrator-Unknown to Molly and Maggie, their mean foster sister was listening outside the door.

Foster Sister-So those little brats think they can have fun, eh? Is that what she thinks? Well, I'll put a stop to that. I can't have any fun if they're having fun. *(Enters room)* Hello sweet, dear sisters.

Molly-What do you want?

Foster Sister-*(Sweetly)* I want to play with you.

Molly-With me?

Foster Sister-Yes. Let's play house.

Maggie-Be careful with those dolls.

Foster Sister-Of course I will be careful. I'm your big sister aren't I? *(Sees Dragon)* What's that supposed to be?

Maggie-He's a fierce dragon!

Foster Sister-*(Sits down behind the dragon and starts to pull the dragon's stuffing out and the dragon slowly slumps over)* Hey look! His stuffings are coming out!

Maggie-Please, don't do that.

Foster Sister-Don't tell me what to do you little brat. Hey Fashion doll. You are so pretty. Can you twist your arm around your head? *(Twists Fashion doll's arm around her face)*

Molly-No!

Foster Sister-*(Approaches Soldier)* Hey Soldier boy! Stand at attention while I'm talking to you! You don't look even. Maybe I will take off the other arm. *(Does so. The child playing the soldier could simply slip his/her arm inside his/her shirt or jacket to simulate that the arm has been removed)* There! That looks so much better! *(Goes to Baby Doll)* Hey Baby! Let me pull your string! *(Pulls the Baby Doll's string repeatedly)*

Baby Doll-*(Starts crawling really fast)* Mama, mama, mama.

Molly-Don't. You'll wear out her batteries!

Foster Sister-*(Pulls the baby's string again)*

Baby Doll-*(Starts to slow down)* Maaa....Maaaaaaa. *(Doll stops)*

Foster Sister- *(Sees Happy Face)* Hey what are you smiling about? *(Approaches Happy Face and pulls his string)*

Happy Face-*(Laughs)*

Foster Sister-Are you laughing at me? *(Pulls string again)*

Happy Face-*(Laughs again)*

Foster Sister-Think you're funny, eh? *(Pulls string again)*

Happy Face-*(Starts laughing slower and slower and then stops)*

Charles Robertson

Foster Sister-You're not so funny now, are you? *(Sees Dancing Doll)* Hey I like that doll. I want to play with it.

Molly-Please don't. She's very delicate. My mother gave it to me before...before...

Foster Sister-Yeah, so what? *(Grabs dancing doll and it crumbles to the ground accompanied by a recorded sound of breaking glass. The doll is broken)* Oops! Gee, I'm sorry. It was likely gonna break anyway. It was so fragile.

Narrator-Something happened that moment in little Molly's heart. It broke. The little dancing doll was all she had left to remind her of her mother. And now it was in pieces.

Molly-*(Hits Foster Sister futiley)* I hate you! I hate you! I hate you!

Maggie-And I hate you too!

Foster Sister-You're in trouble now. Mom! Mom!

Foster Mother-*(Enters)* What is it dear? Oh my! What a mess! What happened?

Foster Sister-*(Starts crying)* Its Molly! She went crazy or something! She started smashing all her dolls. Her and Maggie. I tried to stop them. You know what you always say. Money doesn't grow on trees.

Foster Mother-Exactly right!

Foster Sister-And then they started hitting me *(Starts crying again)* I tried to stop them but they were like wild animals!

Foster Mother-Is that true Molly?

Molly-She's lying! She's lying!

Foster Sister-Who are you going to believe? Me. Your own flesh and blood, or some child that's not even really yours.

Foster Mother-Of course dear. I'll believe you.

Foster Sister-*(Smiles at Molly)*

Foster Mother-*(Grabs a garbage bag and a broom)* Molly! Here's a garbage bag and a broom. I want you to sweep that mess into the garbage!

Molly-No!

Foster Mother-Are you defying me?

Molly-She did it! She broke my dolls!

Foster Mother- Are you calling my little princess *(Puts her arm around the Foster Sister)* a liar?

Maggie-But she is lying!

Foster Sister-See mom. They're all in on it. Its like a conspiracy.

Foster Mother-That's it you two. You're going to bed without any supper!

Molly-But that's not fair!

Foster Mother-Get in that closet!

Molly-What?

Foster Mother-You and Maggie, in that closet now!

Maggie-No, I'm afraid of the dark!

Foster Mother-*(To Foster Sister)* Get the key sweetie. And let's lock them in. That' should teach them some manners.

Molly-I'm sorry. I'll be nice.

Foster Mother-Too late. I have to teach you about respect. Manners. I give you a shelter over your heads, I slave over a hot stove feeding you ungrateful little wretches. I have had it up to here. Up to here. Now, get in there! *(To foster sister)* Sweetie, sweep up that junk and put it in the closet with those brats.

Foster Sister-*(Sweeps up dolls which roll ahead of the broom into the closet-The closet could be off stage)*

Foster Mother-There now give me the key. *(Foster Mother locks the door)* Nightie night night girls.

Foster Sister-Don't let the bed bugs bite.

Maggie- *(From off stage)* Yikes! Are there bed bugs in here?

Narrator-So the mean old Foster Mother and Foster Sister went out to buy stuff for themselves with the money they had received from having Molly and Maggie as foster children, leaving the two girls locked away in the dark. And when children are in the dark sometimes their imaginations can run away with them.

(A simple scene change where the lights grow dimmer or blue gels could suggest darkness-Molly and Maggie could move onstage as if they are exploring the closet. The dolls could move onstage slowly in a very doll-like manner. When they reach center stage they could collapse slowly to the floor. As the scene progresses, the stage could gradually lighten)

Molly-My poor toys.

Maggie-Molly? I'm scared.

Fairy Godmother-Don't worry.

Molly-Who said that?

Fairy Godmother-Don't worry.

Molly-There it is again. Who said that?

Fairy Godmother-I am your...*(A musical flourish)* Fairy Godmother!

Molly-My what?

Fairy Godmother-Your *(Flourish again)* Fairy Godmother!

(The rest of the dolls start coming to life)

Baby Doll-Mama?

Soldier-Excuse me. Could someone find my arm for me? Its a simple operation. Just pop! And its back on.

Molly-Oh, here it is. *(The soldier would have his arm hidden and Molly could mask attaching the arm with her body, blocking the audience's view of what is actually going on)* Just...

Soldier-No anesthetic, just pop...

Molly-Pop? Like this? *(Sticks arm back on)*

Soldier-Yeah, that's it. Now, if only I could find my other arm.

Happy Face-Soldier, you're a wimp. So, you lost an arm. War is tough. What are you gonna do? Cry to your mommy?

Molly-For a Clown, you're not very jolly.

Fashion Doll-Excuse me. I don't mean to interrupt, but all this talk of war and missing arms is making me nauseous.

I have really important problems, like what colour shoes to wear with this outfit. Could you be a doll and move my arm there...

Molly-(*Adjusts Fashion Doll*) There!

Fashion Doll-That's so much more comfortable. Thanks. Thank you very much!

Fairy Godmother-Its dolls like you that have held back the women's movement for so long.

Fashion Doll-Hey, its important to accessorize.

Dragon-Excuse me, does anyone mind if I smoke?

Fashion Doll-Now as if there isn't enough pollution in the world, we have to have fire-breathing dragons.

Molly-Am I imagining all this?

Happy Face-I don't know. It might be your imagination.

Dragon-Its dark in here.

Happy Face-Is the monster scared?

Dragon-I'm not a monster. I'm a dragon.

Happy Face-Whatever.

Baby-I want my mommy.

Fashion Doll-You don't have a mommy stupid. You were born in a factory.

Baby-I thought the stork brought me.

Fairy Godmother-No, it was a truck.

Baby-Aren't I real?

Fashion Doll-No, you're just a doll. We're all dolls except for Molly and Maggie. They're human beings

Baby-Is that like jelly beans?

Dancing Doll-Could somebody help me? I seem to have gone to pieces.

Fairy Godmother-Don't worry I can fix you. Molly, do you have any glue?

Maggie-There should be some inside the toy box.

Baby-I'll go get it. *(Doll crawls toward the toy box)*

Molly-Can you fix her. She's my favourite doll.

Baby-*(Starts chewing on the glue)* Baby eat glue. ..Mmm

Fashion Doll-But I thought I was your favourite doll. I know I'm my favourite doll because I'm so cute.

Molly-Can you fix her?

Fairy Godmother-Of course I can fix her. I am after all; *(Musical flourish)* your fairy godmother! Didn't I fix Cinderella's broken heart?

Maggie-But that was just a story.

Fairy Godmother-And this isn't?

Baby-Mmmm.

Molly-What's wrong with her?

Dragon-I think she glued her lips together.

Fairy Godmother-Soldier boy! Happy Face! We have an emergency here.

Soldier-*(Saluting)* Aye aye sir! Uh, ma'am. Aye aye!

Happy Face-You grab this lip and I'll grab the other.... *(They do as they are told)* Okay, let's pull!

(Ripping Sound)

Happy Face-There!

Soldier-I think we did it. How are you Baby?

Baby-Mmmm. My lips are sore.

Fairy Godmother-*(Applying Glue to Dancing Doll's broken limbs)* There, a little bit of glue there, and a little bit here and Voila! Presto! Abracadabra! She's fixed!

Dancing Doll-*(Slowly stands up, steadies herself and smiles and then sags, her limbs at awkward angles-a badly-glued doll)*

Dragon-What's wrong with her?

Molly-She's all crooked looking.

Dancing Doll-What did you do to me?

Fairy Godmother-I fixed you. What do you want from me? I'm not a doctor.

Dancing Doll-I'll never be able to dance again.

Molly-You ruined my favourite doll!

Dragon-You think you got problems. I got the stuffings knocked out of me.

Fairy Godmother-*(Approaching the Dragon)* Here, I can fix you.

Dragon-*(Pulling away in fear)* No...no. Don't let that quack anywhere near me.

Maggie-*(Approaches the Dragon)* I will fix you. *(Starts stuffing Dragon with his cotton innards-With each addition Dragon straightens out until he is sitting up straight)* There, and there, and there! How's that?

Dragon-*(Smiles)* Thank you. I feel quite...stuffed. Thank you.

Baby-Excuse me. I know I'm just a baby, but I have my needs as well. I'm a bit low on energy. Does anyone have a couple of batteries they can spare?

Fashion Doll-Don't you just hate Malibu Barbie? I mean, just who does she think she is.

Dragon-You all looks the same to me. Identical.

Fashion Doll-Pulease. I have blonde hair. *(Or whichever colour hair the child has)*

Happy Face-Soldier; we have to figure a way out of this mess.

Charles Robertson

Soldier-What do I look like? Wanna see my do a one-armed push-up *(Gets down to try one and fails)*

Happy Face-Wimp!

Maggie-I wish we had a real family.

Molly-Don't worry Maggie. Things will get better. Our foster mother and sister can't help it if they're mean. They don't know any better.

Maggie-*(Starts to cry)*

Molly-Don't cry. We've got to focus. We have to think about how to get out of here.

Soldier-What we need is a plan!

Everybody-*(Gathers around the soldier excitedly)*

Soldier-I didn't say I had a plan. I said we needed one. What we need are reinforcements, the cavalry coming over the hill. Where are the others?

Molly-What others?

Fairy Godmother-The other toys. There must be others.

Molly-I am afraid this is it. We used to have a lot of toys before we moved here. ..before my mother...

Maggie-I miss mommy.

One Act Plays for Kids

Dragon-There there. Pull my string FG.

Fairy Godmother-*(Pulls his string)*

Dragon-*(Sings)* Mister Cuddly is my name. Do you want to play a game?

Maggie-Thanks, but what are we going to do?

Dragon-Hey, don't ask me. I'm just a fierce dragon. I'm practically prehistoric.

Soldier-Has anyone seen my arm?

Happy Face-I think I saw it waving to me from the garbage truck. I think the nice foster sister put it there.

Baby-What's garbage?

Fashion Doll-That's where all the unloved dolls end up.

Baby-Then I'll never grow up! Everyone loves babies.

Happy Face-When our numbers up, we get dumped in with yesterday's news, yesterdays supper, and then we get thrown out on the street corner where the garbage truck takes us away to get recycled. Then we come back in some other form. Its called reincarnation.

Soldier-Yeah, you'll get reincarnated as a fork.

Molly-How are we going to get out of here?

Charles Robertson

Baby-Can I get some batteries here? Double A?

Dragon- I am dragon. Wanna hear me roar?

Fairy Godmother-That's so typical. When in doubt; roar!

Soldier-May I make a suggestion? Maybe we could use our weapons to blast our way out.

Happy Face-Right! Let's lock and load

Soldier*(Pulls out a rifle)* Bang! Bang!

Happy Face-*(Pulls out a Clown gun)* Zoom! Zoom!

Dragon-Nothing seems to be happening!

Fairy Godmother-Use your fire breathing power!

Dragon-*(Sucks in his gut as if to launch a big blast of fire)* Mister Cuddly is my name. Do you want to play a game?

Fairy Godmother-I'll use my magic...Abracadabra!

Baby-I'll help! *(Crawls forward and bumps her head against the door - imaginary or otherwise - without going anywhere)*

Maggie-This just isn't working.

Molly-Maybe the storyteller can get us out of here.

Narrator-Who, me?

Molly-Yeah, you. Can you get us out of here?

Narrator-How would I do that? There are rules you know.
I don't want to get into trouble.

Molly-Please, you're our last hope

Everybody-Please!

Narrator-Okay, okay. I've never actually done this before.
I mean sometimes I tell some pretty rotten stories but I
just keep going, keep plugging ahead. I mean I'm sure
there must be some sort of consequences, but then again.

Fairy Godmother-Oh, would you please just hurry up?

Narrator-Okay, okay. Let me think. Molly and Maggie,
what would you like most of all?

Dancing Doll-I'd like to be able to dance again.

Soldier-I would like another arm.

Fashion Doll-I would like a pink car.

Dragon-I'd like to be a real dragon, and breathe fire and
everything.

Dancing Doll-I would like to be able to dance again.

Narrator-Yes, we heard you.

Baby-And I would like two double A batteries.

Fairy Godmother-And I would like a real magic wand.

Happy Face-And I would like to find my sense of humour.

Narrator-And Molly, Maggie, what would you like?

All-Yeah, you must want something.

Molly-Actually, I would like to live with a real family that loves me.

Dragon-We love you.

Maggie-Can you help us?

Narrator-What do I look like? The Wizard of Oz? Now Molly, Maggie, I suppose, you don't really want to go back home, back to your foster home, do you. You want to live with a real family.

Molly-Yes, oh yes, can you do it?

Narrator-These guys here. They love you. They are your family. Maybe we can get some help.

Molly-From who?

Narrator-*(Indicating audience)* From them. *(Turns to audience)* Hello. As you can see, Molly and Maggie are in a bit of a predicament. They need your help. Kids imaginations, well they can make all sorts of things come to life, even toys. Now we are almost there. We just need a big push from you guys. We need help in the imagination department, a little support. Is everybody ready? Do you believe kids dreams can come true?...Excuse me, I don't think I heard that. Do you believe kids dreams can come true? Somebody forgot their coffee this morning. Do you believe that kids dreams can come true? There. That's so much better! Hit it FG!

Fairy Godmother-But I'm not really magic.

Narrator-Trust me.

Fairy Godmother-Okay, here goes *(Waves her wand)* Zim Zam Zoo!

Dancing Doll-*(Starts to dance)* Look at me! Look at me! I can dance again!

Baby-*(Sniffs air)* Ooh, looks like I'm a real baby now.

Soldier-(*Jumping up and down waving his arms*) My arms! I have arms!

Fashion Doll-What about my car?

Charles Robertson
Fairy Godmother-Cars cause pollution.

Dragon-*(Takes a big breath as if to send out a huge roar but all that he can manage is the same song)* Mister Cuddly is my name. Do you want to play a game?

Fairy Godmother-I guess some things never change.

Happy Face-What did the bee ask the barber? For a buzz cut! Get it! *(Starts laughing uncontrollably)* A buzz cut! *(Rolls around on the floor and everybody freezes)*

Narrator-And of course, they all lived happily ever after. But I suppose you are wondering what happened to the mean foster sister and her mother.

Foster Sister-*(Enters)* Hey you little brats! Where are you? Brats! Hey mom! Molly and Maggie; they're not in their room!

Foster Mom-Remember? We locked them in the closet.

Foster Sister-Oh yeah. *(Knocks on closet door and then opens it)* Hello? Mom! They're not here.

Foster Mom-That's impossible!

Foster Sister-Mom! I think they've run away!

Foster Mom-There goes our foster money. That's the tenth child this year.

Foster Sister-*(Seeing the wand on the floor and bending down to pick it up)* Whats this?

Foster Mom-Looks like some kind of magic wand. Try it out.

Foster Sister-There's no such thing as magic.

Foster Mother-You have no imagination. Try it out!

The Dolls-Try it!

Foster Sister-*(Waves the wand)* I want some new dolls! Zim Zam Zoo! Whatever happens to me, happens to you!

(The Mother and daughter start to stiffen up)

Foster Mother-What's happening?

(They bounce forward at the waist-then they slowly look up-They have been transformed into dolls)

Foster Mother/Sister-Help us!

Narrator-And just about everybody lived happily ever after...

Dancing Doll-Wait a minute? Is that it? I've been doing my part faithfully expecting at any minute to get something interesting to say besides; I can dance...I can't dance. Let me tell you, I'm very disappointed. I'm not a one-

107

dimensional performer. I can do other things besides moving gracefully.

Narrator-I'm sorry but that's all there was for you.

Dancing Doll-But I can act. I'm not just another pretty face. I have feelings, emotions. What did I get?

Three lines? Even the little kid got more lines than me.

Maggie-I got a better agent.

Dancing Doll-I'm a real person with real feelings and emotions, not just some piece of porcelain. I'm an actress. Now, if I don't get more to say, I'm going to march right into the...

Others-*(Grab her while covering her mouth and pulling her back)*

Narrator-Like I said, Just about everybody lived happily ever after. The End

The End

ABOUT THE AUTHOR

Charles Robertson is a playwright and director in Canada
who has been involved in all facets of theatre.
He has written a number of plays for young people,
including *Pretty Pieces, Ghost of the Tree and Three One Act
Comedies for Teens*
With partner Anne Marie Mortensen, he runs
Bottle Tree Productions at www.bottletreeinc.com
Bottle Tree Productions offers free advice and monologues
for aspiring actors.
Bottle Tree Productions' One Act Play Competition for
Writers has a One Thousand Dollar First Prize and closes on
November 30th of each year.

Made in the USA
Monee, IL
12 November 2021

81982321R00066